Inside the Now

Inside the Now

meditations on time

THICH NHAT HANH

PARALLAX
PRESS
Berkeley, California
parallax.org

Parallax Press
P.O. Box 7355
Berkeley, California 94707

Parallax Press is the publishing division of Unified Buddhist Church, Inc.
Printed in Canada

Cover and text design by Jess Morphew
Chinese calligraphy for "being time" on page 140 is by Venerable Kai Ly.
All other calligraphy is by Thich Nhat Hanh.
The brush stroke images on pages 56, 88, and 109 are from iStock.
All other brush stroke images are from Shutterstock.

Library of Congress Cataloging-in-Publication Data

Nhát Hanh, Thích, author.
 Inside the now : meditations on time / Thich Nhat Hanh.
    pages cm
 Summary: "For the first time Thich Nhat Hanh shares his inspiration and experience of living in stillness and timelessness. Written to pull you into the moment as he sees it, Inside the Now offers teachings
inspired by the spirit of poetry. More personal than the majority of his writing, Inside the Now shares
the Zen Master's experience using poetry and meditation to endure and move beyond violence and
oppression. Inspired by Being Time by Zen Master Dogen, Thich Nhat Hanh shares short meditations
along with revelations from his past to give the reader a sense of entering a space of timelessness. In
these meditations, he reveals his own doubts and his own searching."-- Provided by publisher.
 ISBN 978-1-937006-79-2 (hardback)
 1. Time--Religious aspects--Buddhism. 2. Spiritual life--Buddhism. 3. Meditation--Buddhism. I. Title.
 BQ9800.T5392N45446 2015
 294.3'442--dc23
                                2015034198

1 2 3 4 5 / 19 18 17 16 15

Contents

Preface

*I*nside *the Now* is a book in two parts: the first is an autobiographical prologue *(The Way In)* and the second is a profound contemplation on time, love, and happiness *(Now I See)*. Thich Nhat Hanh wrote this book in the summer of 2013, while he was staying at the European Institute of Applied Buddhism in Waldbröl, Germany.

Now I See is an extended free verse poem about time and what it means to be fully present in the here and now. Thay, (as Thich Nhat Hanh is known to his students) takes as his inspiration a series of lines about the passing of time from Vietnam's most famous epic poem, *The Tale of Kiều*, in the same way that the thirteenth-century Japanese Zen

Master Dōgen took lines from an earlier Chinese poem as the inspiration for his own great contemplation on time, "Being Time," (Uji, 有時).

For many readers, this will be the first encounter with *The Tale of Kiều*, an historical tale that is part romance and part tragedy, set in a medieval era of Confucianism and warlords. It is the story of a beautiful young woman, Kiều, who experiences great love but also suffers immense misfortune and hardship. It is Kiều's love and her suffering that lead her, ultimately, to deep understanding and insight. Thay has selected a few vivid moments from *The Tale of Kiều* that reveal something universal about our experience of time, love, and happiness. For readers who are interested, a brief plot summary of *The Tale of Kiều* and context for the quotes are provided in the Notes.

You may have already experienced how in moments of a strong feeling of love—whether it is the love of deep friendship, the love between parents and children, or the love of an intimate relationship—you touch "the now" with greater vividness and intensity. When you can look into a loved one's eyes, hold one another close, and see and know one another completely, you may feel that time stands still.

In *Now I See* Thay shows us how any moment, including a moment experienced alone with our wonderful planet, can have this same intensity and quality of deep love and connection. Each and every moment is already more beautiful than we could ever have imagined. We just need to learn how to see it.

Now I See begins by establishing that there is no such thing as a heaven where everything is pure and blissful. As Thay has often taught, there cannot be a lotus without the mud. In the same way, we cannot have happiness without suffering: happiness is born from understanding and transforming suffering. The wonderful present moment is, therefore, a place where we know how to embrace and understand our suffering and difficulties. Using the eloquent poetry of *The Tale of Kiều*, as well as that of renowned Zen masters and his own poetry, Thay shows us how important it is to come back to the now in order to truly cultivate joy, take care of suffering, and generate understanding, love, compassion, and insight.

Perhaps Thay was inspired by *The Tale of Kiều* because Kiều's suffering resonates closely with the suffering that he and his loved ones experienced in Vietnam under decades of colonialism, occupation, violence, and war. *Now I See* is a kind of lotus that has bloomed from the mud of that suffering.

After completing the manuscript for *Now I See*, Thay wrote the autobiographical introduction, which he called *The Way In*. It is a "prequel" to *Now I See*, describing his years in Vietnam from 1949 until his exile in 1966. These were challenging and formative years for Thay, as a young monk, poet, scholar, and community-builder struggling to develop in Vietnam a Buddhism relevant to the suffering of his time.

Thay shares intimately about his deep interconnection with his fellow monks and poets, teachers, friends, and students; and we learn how poetry, writing, art, and the close bonds of brotherhood and sisterhood nourished and sustained their spirits. Thay introduces us to those who inspired him, those who supported him, and those whose lives were taken by the ravages of war. The intense experiences of life, love, and loss described in *The Way In* shine light on the insights into time and interbeing presented in *Now I See*. Thay's autobiographic writing reveals how understanding, love, compassion, and insight are not abstract ideas, but energies which can be generated in real-life situations, no matter how difficult they may be.

In *The Way In* Thay shows us how poetry can be both a song of insight and an eloquent voice for change. When one of Thay's poems was first published in *The New York Review of Books* in 1966, it dominated the front page and helped foster a national discussion about the terrible costs of war. His indefatigable efforts to write bravely and eloquently, sometimes at the risk of his own life, can inspire us to discover ways to contribute a spiritual voice to the issues of our own times—to the challenges of war and violence, hatred and discrimination, and the devastation of our beautiful planet.

In the decades since 1966, Thay has developed, from his roots in Vietnamese Zen, profoundly effective practices of mindfulness and meditation that go beyond boundaries of nationality and faith, to touch peace and healing, and cultivate compassion and insight. If in the 1950s and '60s he was tirelessly searching, in *Now I See* he reveals, with profound simplicity and eloquence, what he was looking for and what he has found.

There is no separation between Thay's spirituality, his poetry, and his deep aspiration to engage with and transform the suffering in the world. Just as his early, profoundly spiritual poems and writings called for change in Vietnam, so too does this new poetic contemplation, *Now I See*, call for deep, personal transformation in each one of us who reads it.

This book reveals two different voices: the voice and poetry of Thay as a young monk in *The Way In*, and the clear and direct voice of a Zen master in *Now I See* as he challenges us to open our hearts, seize the moment, and truly touch the now.

We hope that this deeply personal and intimate journey of spiritual discovery will show you the way to touch the now so deeply that you will be able to see who you really are, see those you truly love, and together touch the ultimate.

Sister True Dedication
Plum Village, 2015

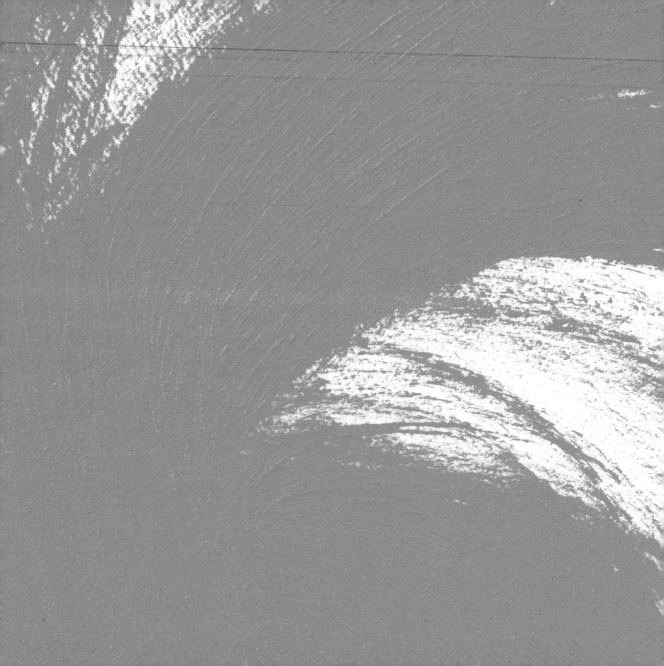

The Way In

Poetic Inspiration

For Thích Nhất Hạnh

As a bridge of sympathy between Spirituality and Poetry

From Trụ Vũ

My head cushioned on illusory dreams

I carry the soul of poetry in the garment of heaven and earth

Sleeping amidst fallen autumn leaves

Ground surges up to touch sky

Who let autumn recede into the distance?

What is that song rising from the sea?

Who painted grey clouds on the canvas of space?

One golden leaf falling, is enough to disturb my heart

As I hold in my hand the seasons of creation

And befriend earth and sky

Life sleeps deeply under my feet

Body bound tight under ancient earth

From a thousand directions comes wind of sky and sea

Blowing far and high the wings of a solitary bird

I return, at one with emptiness

The poet's inspiration will endure a thousand years . . .

—Trụ Vũ

When I was twenty-three years old, I met two impoverished young poets, Trụ Vũ and Quách Thoại, at the Source of Awakening Temple in the port district of Saigon, where I was living as a young monk. It was the autumn of 1949, and for three years our whole country had been engulfed in a terrible war between the French colonial forces struggling to reclaim the country for France, and the resistance fighters battling to win Vietnam's independence.

The poets had come to live at the temple and teach Vietnamese literature to the novices, in order to have somewhere to stay and something to eat. The Dragon River Press had recently agreed to publish a collection of my poems, *Reed Flute in the Autumn Twilight*. It was my first book. They had given me fifty author copies as payment, which I shared amongst my friends, so I didn't have any left to offer to our two young poets.

Then, one afternoon I was out teaching novices at the Responsive Radiance Temple, on the road the French colonists called Rue de Lorgeril, when Trụ Vũ came in looking for me. He had found a copy of *Reed Flute in the Autumn Twilight* at the Dragon River Press, and had taken it to Tao Đàn Garden to lie down on the grass and read. He fell asleep and upon waking, the poem "Poetic Inspiration" came to him. He went straight to find me and offer it to me. Born of this heartfelt exchange, a profound connection developed between us.

Trụ Vũ prefaced the poem with the following dedication: *"For Thích Nhất Hạnh—As a bridge of sympathy between Spirituality and Poetry."* But, I wondered, is such a bridge really necessary?

Isn't poetry already spirituality, and spirituality already poetry?

A few months later, in my collection of poems *The Golden Light of Spring*, I included two lines on the interconnection and deep interbeing of poetry and Buddhism in a passage about the Buddha's passing:

May the radiant light of the golden path—source of poetry—

Illumine the depths of the darkest night.

Song of Eternity

Of the two poets, we didn't see Quách Thoại as much as Trụ Vũ. Although his writing revealed a strong and bold spirit, his physical constitution was weak, and within a few years he had succumbed to tuberculosis. Amongst his manuscripts we found the following poem, "A Dahlia Flower," which touched me deeply:

Standing quietly by the fence,

you smile your wondrous smile.

I am speechless, and my senses are filled

by the sound of your beautiful song,

beginningless and endless.

I bow deeply to you.

A few years later, Quách Thoại's beautiful, miraculous flower reappeared in my poem "April":

. . . The sun is up.

One of your tiny petals carries a dewdrop

imitating the sun, shining forth.

The forest doesn't seem to know you are there,

although you have already begun to sing your immortal song.

A song that sounds as if it has been there forever

in the solemn atmosphere of the deep forest . . .

The Golden Path

When I was young, two of the principal sources of my inspiration to become a monk were the Zen Master Mật Thể and the author Nguyễn Trọng Thuật, who wrote the celebrated book *The Watermelon*, one of the first novels ever written in Vietnamese. Nguyễn Trọng Thuật also wrote a deeply inspiring history of the Zen lineage in Vietnam, which was serialized in the *Torch of Wisdom* magazine. Zen Master Mật Thể was a brilliant scholar, with a great vision for the future of Buddhism. His seminal book *The Spring of Ethics* was published in 1942, the year I became a novice. In it, Mật Thể advocated that Buddhism's mission should be to bring about "a new spring" for our country. He believed that Buddhist spirituality and ethics could open a new path that would liberate humanity from the depths of doubt, despair, and depravity. Of all my elders, he was the one I felt closest to in my deep desire to become a monk. He too wrote poetry—poetry that was very gentle and pure.

The moon is shining after the rain
The yard fragrant with perfumed breeze
The bell resounds in the evening silence
Asking whose souls have awakened

—Zen Master Mật Thể

Thầy Mật Thể ordained at the age of twelve at the Bamboo Forest Monastery in Huế. At that time, Miss Đạm Phương, one of Vietnam's first feminists and an important writer, used to come to the temple to teach the monks literature, as well as the modern Vietnamese script. In those days, many monks could read and write better in Sino-Vietnamese, using Chinese characters, than with the new system, using the roman alphabet. But as Thầy Mật Thể had already mastered both Vietnamese and Chinese, he was able to learn French, which then allowed him to read the most up-to-date Buddhist research being published by French scholars. He later studied at the Xiao Shan Buddhist Institute in China, and even before receiving the *bhikshu* precepts, he had already become a respected professor of Buddhism and a published scholar on the history of Buddhism in Vietnam.

The Heart of Eternity

I feel very fortunate that, as a monastic, I have been close to many wonderful elder and younger brothers. We loved one another even more than we loved our own blood brothers. We lived, studied, and practiced together happily in the spirit of true and wonderful brotherhood. We all loved Buddhism and we all loved our country. All of us wanted to contribute something, whether great or small, to help resist the French occupation. Many of us shared a deeply rooted faith that it should be possible to create a kind of Buddhism that would respond to the needs of our country, that could be applied in daily life, and that could liberate us from our suffering.

Yet for eight years, from 1946 to 1954, the war with the French—"the dirty war," as Jean Paul Sartre would call it—continued to rage around us. The walls of our temple in Huế were riddled with bullet holes; and each day when night would come, the ambience of war and death would return. The sound of gunfire and explosions could be heard in all directions, and bullets flew over our roof. French soldiers would raid our temples, searching for resistance fighters or food, demanding that we hand over the last of our rice.

Monks were killed, even though they were unarmed. My elder brother, Trí Thuyên, was shot dead by the French in the Diamond Mountain Pagoda. Several of my fellow novices, close friends I had studied with at the Báo Quốc Institute of Buddhist Studies in Huế, were also killed. My younger brother, Tâm Thường, was shot dead on the Mountain of the Immortals, right beside the Zen Lineage Temple. Young Minh Tâm was shot while out in the rural district of Phong Điền, and young Tánh Huyền was shot behind the Auspicious Cloud Temple. Brother Châu Quang was shot right in the city center of Huế . . .

We secretly organized memorial ceremonies for our brothers. We kept a portrait of Thầy Trí Thuyên and, below it, these four lines by Thầy Trọng Ân:

In ancient times were we not together
Lighting the fragrant brazier, vowing under the tower of clarity?
But now, with the land still not at peace
Where do you wander lost? Your image here endures.

On the anniversary of the death of our younger brother Tâm Thường, I wrote this poem:

Tâm Thường, my friend, in this early morning mist,

Can you hear the wind calling amongst the thousand pines?

On the Mountain of the Immortals, the ancient pagoda is obscured

Clouded by gunsmoke and the haze of war

Have you seen the bluebird land by the forest

Uttering without cease its grief-stricken cry?

When will it ever stop?

Do you hear the heroic strains of music

Full of noblest will and strongest resolve?

The source of poetic inspiration rises

as a joyous cry from centuries past.

In spirit, at the source of the sublime way,

One path, two aspirations raised together

We go on . . . Remember the spring evenings of years gone by

When everyone gathered together

Around the warm hearth, fragrant with sandalwood.

We go out . . . Tender blows the wind over mountains and rivers

Spring falls on a thousand radiant trees

The forceful call of the spirit rises in tumult:

"Out now, go! The darkness has prevailed too long,

Find the ancient ruins hidden under the distant ocean!

Bring back the light to the places of shadow!"

We step out, hearts still young and full of elation

Look at the floating clouds, and the far-off misty mountains and rivers.

On the long path, I am impassioned

"The heart of that day will be the heart of eternity."

My friend, the mirror of time was never broken

In the heart of anyone. The source of life is infinite still.

This evening, lighting the incense, the smoke surges up,

Go, my friend, and visit those who dwell in the undiscovered country!

"The heart of that day will be the heart of eternity" are the words of the vow we chose to patiently pursue, and the ideal of service by which we swore to live. We knew that the spirit of poetic inspiration, the heart of spirituality, and the mind of love could not be extinguished by death. If those who went ahead were cut down, then those who followed would continue them.

Around 1950, three of us young monks who had been living at the Source of Awakening Temple in Saigon moved out to Vietnam's central highlands to start a community of young monastics at the Miraculous Brightness Pagoda on the Dalat plateau. We had a deep need to come together with others to nourish ourselves, and were eagerly searching for a way to make Buddhism relevant to the immediate needs of the people. There, with the wholehearted support of the young abbot, we established an Institute of Buddhist Studies for monks and nuns, and set up a new middle school and primary school for children—the first private Buddhist schools in Vietnam run by monastics.

A New Spring

Finally, after a decisive defeat at the battle of Điện Biên Phủ in 1954, the French were forced to surrender their colonies in Vietnam. The three-month-long Geneva Conference concluded with a treaty declaring a cease-fire and the division of the country into North and South. The news that the country would be partitioned shook the whole population. Many young monastics were in a state of shock and confusion. In 1954 the new Buddhist administration of South Vietnam called me back from the central highlands to Saigon, and asked me to help renew and modernize the program of studies and practice for the young generation of monks and nuns. In addition to the classes, we soon set up a student association and began publishing a magazine called *The New Lotus Season*. We initiated the "Engaged Buddhism" movement, having first introduced the term in a series entitled *A New Perspective on Buddhism*, which was featured on the front page of *The Democrat* newspaper. We wanted to offer a new kind of Buddhism—a Buddhism that could act as a raft, to save the whole country from the desperate situation of conflict, division, and war.

I was a young Dharma teacher and my students in Saigon were just like my younger brothers and sisters. We shared a common vision and purpose and, even now, whenever I think of them, I still feel so much gratitude—for the love between teacher and student, and for the spirit of brotherhood and sisterhood that we shared. This love has endured, and our intimate friendship has been able to nourish every other kind of love. Looking back today, I am very grateful to have always had a good connection with the younger generation.

The spirit of our Engaged Buddhism was the continuation of Zen Master Mật Thể's vision, but it was still too radical for the majority of the elders in the Buddhist establishment. They dismissed many of our ideas, and steadily began to silence our voices. We felt at a loss. We were young, we had no position or temple of our own. How could we realize our dreams? Still, we refused to give up hope. We continued to write articles, publish books, and sow the seeds of a new kind of unified Buddhism that could respond to the needs of the people, and the needs of our time.

Within a few years, Zen Master Mật Thể passed away. He was only forty-nine. Although he was not able to realize his dream in his lifetime, that dream lived on in us, and lives on in us still. After his passing, I took on his only disciple, Thầy Châu Toàn, whom I loved as a younger brother. Perhaps I loved him even more than a blood brother, because we shared the same dream and aspiration. This was true with all my other brothers. It's strange, but we were never angry with each other and we never quarrelled—perhaps because we had such deep faith in one another.

Forest Refuge

During those difficult years, together with a number of close friends and students, I did everything I could to create a grassroots Buddhism that could respond to the challenges of the times; offering chants and prayers was not enough to stop the war. But we were accused of sowing seeds of dissent, our magazines were eventually closed down, and the setbacks we were facing in the struggle for peace wore us down. It was then that some of us suddenly had the idea of building a practice center, a place of refuge to nourish and heal ourselves after periods of intense activity. It would be a chance for us to develop concrete Buddhist practices to offer to the people of our country, to heal our wounds, refresh our spirits, and give all of us the strength we needed to continue to help change the situation.

In August 1957 we sought and found some land in the mountainous Đại Lão Forest, a remote and quiet place with plenty of space, clear streams, and paths for walking. I remember the very first time I drove up the dirt road into the deep and mysterious forest. I was with Sister Diệu Âm, our fearless and compassionate elder sister, who actively supported our vision with immense faith and trust. In that moment, as we saw the forest for the first time, I knew we were seeing the future. There we established Phương Bối (the Fragrant Palm Leaves Hermitage), and gradually began to develop it into a practice community. We had the idea of planting persimmon trees and selling the fruit to sustain the community, and we planned to call it Persimmon Village.

But within four years we were forced to abandon our refuge and scatter once more to the winds. The government suspected us of clandestine activities and made it impossible for us to stay. Some of us fled to Saigon and others were forced into a strategic hamlet nearby, set up by government troops for "protection."

Our Plum Village Practice Center in France is a new manifestation of the spirit of Phương Bối. So too was Bát Nhã Monastery, which was established in the hills not far from Phương Bối. There, from 2005 to 2009, over four hundred of my young Vietnamese monastic disciples built a thriving community of practice. Although the government—fearing the monastery's growing popularity—shut it down in 2009 and forcibly disbanded the community, the young Bát Nhã monks and nuns continue to embody the spirit of both Bát Nhã and Phương Bối in our practice centers all over the world.

Poetry for Peace

In 1964, I was invited to become editor in chief of the new weekly magazine *The Sound of the Rising Tide,* the official publication of the newly established Vietnamese Unified Buddhist Church in Saigon. I asked my younger brother Thầy Châu Toàn to be editorial secretary, and he in turn invited the acclaimed poet Vũ Hoàng Chương to be responsible for the poetry pages. At that time we had also just established Fragrant Palm Leaves Press, which was already publishing many influential books by scholars and artists in the capital.

Vũ Hoàng Chương had recently published the poem "Fire of Compassion" in honor of Venerable Thích Quảng Đức, our revered elder whose love, courage, and hope was so great that he set himself on fire in order to call the world's attention to the suffering of the Vietnamese people. Vũ Hoàng Chương was something of a poet laureate for the South, and although he later became widely known for his "drunken poetry" and passionate, inebriated lifestyle, Buddhism was still his primary inspiration. His poems of the 1960s, written when we were all collaborating on the magazine, were infused with the purity, hope, and peace of meditation.

> *Buddha's heart stirs with love for this life of sorrow.*
> *Transforming his body into snow falling from the four quarters,*

He becomes a lotus of one hundred petals, a thousand-meter tree.

All bitterness soothed away by a single drop of stillness.

The Sound of the Rising Tide soon began reporting on the Buddhist community's efforts to bring about peace and reunify the country. Vũ Hoàng Chương would provide poems to accompany the photos and news. He and Thầy Châu Toàn worked very closely and they would go together to gather news about the monks' ongoing hunger strike at the Vietnam National Temple (Quốc Tự) in protest against the government's oppression. From time to time, when Vũ Hoàng Chương came over to visit us at the Bamboo Forest Monastery, he would also bring us a poem. Vũ Hoàng Chương was outspoken and defiant—qualities that would cost him his freedom and his life within a few months of the Communist regime coming to power in 1975.

During the time we were all working on the magazine in Saigon, I was living in a little thatched hermitage in the grounds of the Bamboo Forest Monastery, about an hour's motorbike ride from the city center. Thầy Châu Toàn was also living there, and every day he would travel in to the magazine offices by moped. The abbot Thầy Đồng Bổn, Thầy Châu Toàn, and I had all been novices together in Huế twenty years earlier. My two brothers made the monastery into a wonderful, happy place for us all to take refuge in. Thầy Châu Toàn was truly an artist and had a real talent for making beautiful flower arrangements, and Thầy Đồng Bổn was an excellent cook and would often treat us to his famous green jackfruit dish. Every week we would come together to practice sitting meditation, walking meditation, Dharma discussion, and silent meals, and we would imagine the future together. Many university students—including sister Phượng, who later became Sister Chân Không—would also join us and sometimes ask me to recite poetry for them.

It was around this time that the pioneering literary journal *Creativity* launched "free poetry" (*poésie libre*), a kind of poetry that broke free from the very strict traditional rules of meter and rhyme. My poems on war and peace, many of which were also written in free verse, were being published in the poetry pages of *The Sound of the Rising Tide.* When a collection was printed in 1965, government police came to seize them from the bookstores, but they had all already been sold. They were read and heard by many Vietnamese people, and sometimes they were sung with guitar accompaniment at student meetings, just as songs of protest were being sung in the United States. Many of them were denounced as "anti-war poems"—interestingly by both sides fighting in the war.

The Sound of the Rising Tide soon became the most popular Buddhist weekly in Vietnam. Fifty thousand copies were printed every week, and they were delivered by plane to Huế and Danang to meet demand. We heard that our esteemed poetry editor Vũ Hoàng Chương had remarked how strange it was that my "peace poems" in *The Sound of the Rising Tide* were by far the best poems of the free poetry movement, even though I never said they were "free poetry."

The lines below are typical of those poems—they are excerpted from "Our Green Garden," which was translated into English and published in *The New York Review of Books* in 1966.

Fires spring up like dragon's teeth at the ten points of the universe.

A furious acrid wind sweeps them toward us from all sides.

Aloof and beautiful, the mountains and rivers abide.

All around, the horizon burns with the color of death.

As for me, yes, I am still alive,

But my body and the soul in it writhe as if they too had been set afire.

My parched eyes can shed no more tears.

Where are you going this evening, dear brother, in what direction?

The rattle of gunfire is close at hand.

In her breast, the heart of our mother shrivels and fades like a dying flower.

She bows her head, the smooth black hair now threaded with white.

How many nights, night after night, has she crouched wide awake,

Alone with her lamp, praying for the storm to end?

Dearest brother, I know it is you who will shoot me tonight,

Piercing our mother's heart with a wound that can never heal.

O terrible winds that blow from the ends of the Earth

To hurl down our houses and blast our fertile fields!

I say farewell to the blazing, blackening place where I was born.

Here is my breast! Aim your gun at it, brother, shoot!

I offer my body, the body our mother bore and nurtured.

Destroy it if you will,

Destroy it in the name of your dream,

That dream in whose name you kill.

Can you hear me invoke the darkness:

"When will these sufferings end,

O darkness, in whose name you destroy?"

Come back, dear brother, and kneel at our mother's feet.

Don't make a sacrifice of our dear green garden

To the ragged flames that are carried into the front yard

By wild winds from far away.

Here is my breast. Aim your gun at it, brother, shoot!

Destroy me if you will

And build from my carrion whatever it is you are dreaming of.

Who will be left to celebrate a victory made of blood and fire?

In 1964, the same year I began editing *The Sound of the Rising Tide*, we also established the School of Youth for Social Service (SYSS) and founded Vạn Hạnh University. Our vision for the university was to revive the open-minded spirit of the educational system of Vietnam's ancient dynasties, to free young minds from dogmatic studies, and to teach them the qualities of understanding, love, and trust that could save our country.[1] We assigned a different brother to lead each branch of our work. One elder brother became rector of the university; another the director of Fragrant Palm Leaves Press; another, Thầy Thanh Văn, became director of the SYSS; and my young brother Thầy Châu Toàn continued to be editor of *The Sound of the Rising Tide* magazine. Thầy Thanh Văn became director of the SYSS when he was only twenty-four years old. He was a very gentle and very brave young monk, and directed with deep insight, calm, and compassion, the thousands of young people working in our village reconstruction programs. When he was accidentally killed by a drunk American soldier driving a military truck, Thầy Châu Toàn was asked to take over as the director of the SYSS.

But within barely two years of starting all these initiatives, I was exiled from Vietnam for daring to publicly call for a cease-fire and peace negotiations. It was the summer of 1966. The SYSS began facing significant financial and legal difficulties, and we had to struggle from a distance to mobilize support in order to help the school continue. The SYSS had already realized many remarkable projects: offering relief for war victims; taking care of orphans of the war; establishing villages for victims of the war so that they would have a fixed place to live; and building locally administered "pilot" villages to demonstrate the ability of the people to self-organize.

I can now see clearly that everything that came to be was a continuation, a new manifestation, of what had come before. The Bamboo Forest Monastery in Saigon, our refuge and base during our years of intense activity in the 1960s, was the continuation of the Bamboo Forest Monastery in Huế, where we had studied and practiced as novices in the 1940s under the inspiring presence of Thầy Mật Thể. My beloved younger brother Thầy Châu Toàn, with his sincere heart of service, was the continuation of his teacher, Thầy Mật Thể, who had been the first to give us the vision that such an engaged Buddhism was even possible. You cannot take Thầy Mật Thể out of Thầy Châu Toàn, nor either of them out of me. We inter-are. The same is true for all my elder and younger brothers, and for each one of my students.

Exiled from my country, I could not be present the day that Thầy Thanh Văn passed away. The day Thầy Châu Toàn passed away I also could not be present. It was only in 2005 that I was allowed to return to Vietnam, after forty years had slipped away. I offered incense for both of them at the Bamboo Forest Monastery and at the Floating Cloud Temple.

Today all of us are continued in our younger generation of monastics, present all around the world. We are continued, too, in our poetry.

Love, Poetry, and Time

Nguyễn Du (1766–1820) is perhaps the greatest of all Vietnamese poets. His epic poem *The Tale of Kiều* holds a special place in the hearts of the Vietnamese people, and even illiterate farmers can still recite entire passages from memory. For many Vietnamese now living, *The Tale of Kiều* has become a powerful metaphor for the suffering of the Vietnamese people and their homeland.

The tale is the story of a highly intelligent, talented, and beautiful, but desperately unlucky young woman named Kiều, who endures fifteen years of tragedy and misfortune. Twice she is forced into prostitution and twice into servitude. Yet despite encountering immense hardship, suffering, and despair, she is able again and again to find the strength to trust in the power of love. And it is this deep love—not only for her family, for her first love Kim Trọng, and for the rebel hero Từ Hải, but also for many thousands of soldiers whose lives she spares at a terrible cost to herself—that eventually leads her to peace.[2]

Nguyễn Du vividly captures intense moments of understanding and insight between Kiều and her lovers. I read Nguyễn Du when I was still young, and was very surprised that such an imposing and solemn Confucian scholar could write such ardent and romantic lines of poetry, expressing all the passion, the recklessness, and the folly of youth. Nguyễn Du witnessed the ugliest and most hateful aspects of a corrupt society undergoing total collapse, but at the same time he was able to see that poetry embodying the virtues of beauty, nobility, and spiritual purity could perhaps help save even such a society from disaster.

The many and varied words that Nguyễn Du uses in *The Tale of Kiều* to describe the experience of time, gave rise to the inspiration to write the following poetic contemplation, *Now I See*. It is a deep meditation on time, love, and happiness. Dear friends, please read just one short section at a time, exactly as you would if you were reading *Being Time*, by the great Zen Master Dōgen.[3]

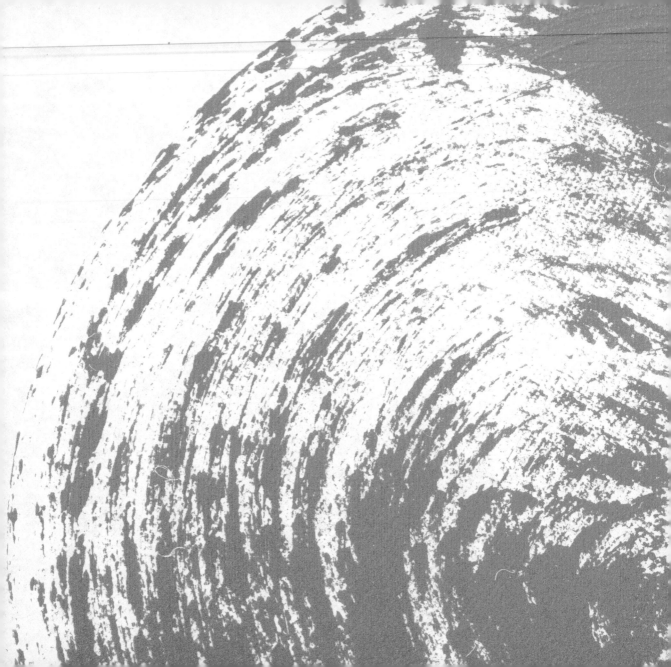

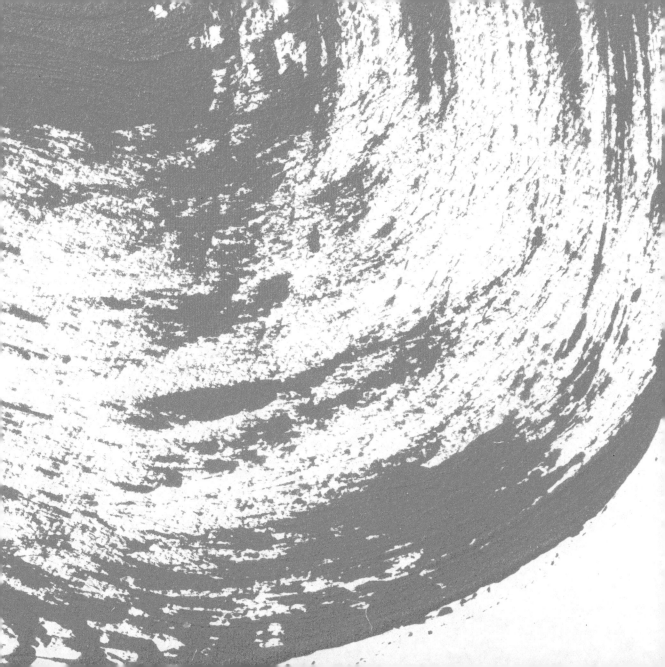

Now I See

now

i see

For so long until now, I could not see. Why not? I may have been searching for a long time, but I couldn't yet see. Perhaps it's because I'm not searching anymore that I now begin to see. And what is it that I see? What is it that I've been searching for?

Maybe what I've been searching for is myself. I want to know who I am. I want to know: *Who* is the one practicing meditation? *Who* is the one trying to look deeply? *Who* is the one reciting the Buddha's name?

有土即非淨

言詮何所爲？

佛說原無我

禅師問是誰？

Polin Temple

Lantau Island, Hong Kong

Zen Masters and Pure Lands

Fifty years ago, on the wall of Polin Temple on Lantau Island, Hong Kong, I saw this poem:

> *If there is a Land, then it cannot be described as Pure.*
>
> *What is the use of words and expressions?*
>
> *If the Buddha says there is no self*
>
> *Who then is the Zen master?*

There is no such thing as a Pure Land. If there is life in that land, then that land cannot really be called pure. People in such a Pure Land have to eat, and if they eat, they have to defecate. In that land, there must be meditation halls, dining halls, and also toilets. If there are toilets, then it is no longer pure. So as soon as

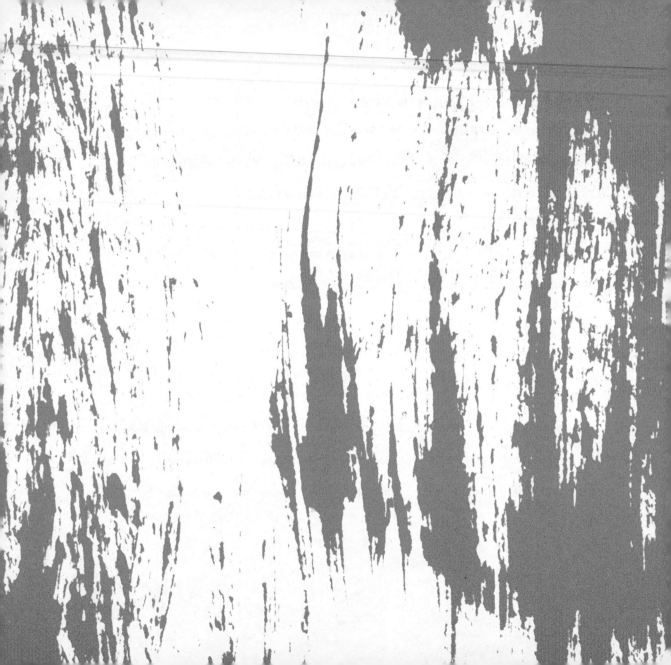

you say the two words "Pure Land," you are wrong. *What then is the use of words and expressions?* Yet followers of the Pure Land school of Buddhism believe that reciting the Buddha's name over and over again will help them be reborn in the Pure Land, a kind of beautiful Kingdom of Heaven, after they die.

If you are looking for a Pure Land or a Kingdom of Heaven to go to after you die, then you are caught. If you follow the Zen school of Buddhism, and you think you need to look for a master from whom to receive transmission, you are equally caught.

If what the Buddha taught about nonself is true, then who is the Zen master? Is the Zen master who is teaching you a self? Who are you? Who is the Zen master? The Buddha has made it very clear: there is no self. Who is the one reciting the Buddha's name? It is me. Yet I do not really know who I am—that is why I am searching for myself.

"Who is the one reciting the Buddha's name?" is a koan.[4] At first it may seem that I already know who the Buddha is, but what I don't yet know is who I am. In fact, if I really knew who the Buddha was, then I would already know who I am. I have been searching for the Buddha. And I have been searching for myself. Only now that I have stopped searching, do I begin to see.

Back to the Now

Where was I looking for the Buddha? Where was I looking for myself? Somewhere in the past? In the future? But the past is already gone and the future is not yet here. Past and future are both illusions. They are only ideas. Only the present is real. Only the now is real. That is why I have to come back to the now if I want to really see the Buddha and really see myself.

We can see it only if we go back to the now.
It is that simple.

The now is the only moment when and where you can find what you have been looking for. You have been searching for Nirvana. You have been looking for God. You have been looking for enlightenment, for awakening. You have been looking for the Pure Land, and for your true nature of no birth and no death.

It turns out that everything you have been looking for
is already there in the present moment.
And the secret of the finding is to go back to the now.

only now
do i see

Only Now Do I See

Only now do I see, is part of a line from *The Tale of Kiều* by Nguyễn Du, Vietnam's most well-known epic poem. It can be translated literally as: *arriving in the now, I see the here.* Only in *the now* can you see *the here.*

The here represents space, and *the now* represents time. *The now* is encountering *the here.* Is it possible to detach *the here* from *the now*? Is it possible to take space out of time? Are they two different things, or are they the same thing?

> *Only now do I see what is here before me,*
>
> *Yet from the first my heart had seen for sure the days to come.*[5]

Kiều is addressing the rebel warrior Từ Hải, her great love, as he returns to her after a long year away with a huge new army under his command.

He is now a man of great power and fortune, a rebel king. This does not surprise Kiều. It is not only now that she can see who he really is; she could already see his greatness and heroic future the very first time they met. "When I first saw you, even though I had not yet seen you as a king, I already knew you were a king. I didn't need to see you with a hundred thousand soldiers at your command to really know who you were. I could see them in your future, and I was sure of what I saw."

It is obvious that when you look deeply into the now, you can already see the future. That is why *the now* and *the here* are so important. Looking deeply into *the here* and *the now* you can see all the ten directions as well as the past, the present, and the future. The ten directions *are* the three times themselves. The poet understood that we have to come back to *the now* in order to see *the here*, and coming back to *the here* allows us to see *the now.* Arriving in the now, I see the here. Isn't this truly wonderful?

現法

Time Itself

现法, *hiện pháp* in Vietnamese, or *dṛṣṭādharma* in Sanskrit, means "that which is now being seen." That which is now being seen is *time itself*. That which is being seen is the present moment—it is the now.

What you see is yourself.

Life Itself

What is there that you see? First of all, it is your body, the miraculousness of which we have not even begun to measure: these two shining eyes capable of beholding moon and stars, these two legs, still strong enough to climb a mountain.

How many such wonders have you not yet truly seen?

You know that you have a body, but when you busy yourself with your computer for hours on end, you completely forget that you have a body.

When you remember to breathe in and out mindfully, your mind comes back to your body and back to the present moment, back to the now. In the present moment, the first thing you encounter is your body. Getting in touch with your body you see the history of life—you see your parents and your ancestors in you, not only human ancestors but also animal, plant, and mineral ancestors. They are all alive and fully present in every cell of your body. You can also see your spiritual ancestors in you. You can see Mother Earth and Father Sun in you.

Looking into your body, you will discover that you are not a separate self, cut off from everything else, but that you are a continuously flowing stream—the stream of life itself.

Your Body Encompasses the Whole Cosmos

To see a World in a Grain of Sand

And a Heaven in a Wild Flower,

Hold Infinity in the palm of your hand,

And Eternity in an hour.[6]

The one contains the all. Your body can tell you everything there is to know about the cosmos, boundless space, and time without end. You will see that *the here* is also *the there*, and that *the now* carries within itself the span of eternity, including the past and the future. Eternity is there to be touched in each moment. Both sun and moon, all the stars and all the black holes, can nestle comfortably inside a tiny grain of sand.

The entire cosmos can sing to us

with the voice of a wild flower.

Finding Each Other in the Now

In the now we see each other clearly,

Outside of this moment, will everything be remembered

only as a dream? [7]

From the very first moment they see each other, Kiều and the handsome scholar Kim Trọng fall desperately in love, but the customs of Confucian society of that time make it very difficult for them to meet. Kim Trọng moves to a house close by and eventually they arrange to meet secretly when Kiều's family is out. They are able to spend a single magical afternoon together. Kiều returns home at dusk, before her family can discover her absence. Finding her family has not yet returned, she cannot resist going back to be with Kim Trọng a little longer. Under the light of the rising moon, she creeps out once more, and the sound of her footsteps on the gravel path wakes Kim Trọng. In his half-sleeping, bewildered state, he asks whether he is dreaming or if she has really come back. Kiều's reply reveals deep insight: *"In this moment*, I am seeing you, and you are seeing me; but," she says, "who knows whether *outside of this moment* everything will be no more than a dream?"

Only in the here and the now do we have a chance to see each other clearly. Outside of the now there is only illusion. The now carries within itself true life, along with all its wonders. Your beloved is one of those wonders. It is only in the frame of the now that you can recognize the presence of your beloved.

Do you possess the now? If you don't have the now, how can you love? This is why every breath and every step that you make must bring you back to the now. If you don't have the now, then you don't have anything—not even yourself; everything is, and will be, no more than a dream.

It is only in the now that we can recognize
each other's presence. Outside of the now, everything
is as insubstantial as smoke.

The first time he met Kiều, the warrior Từ Hải invited her to come close to him, to see him clearly:

Come here, come close, and look again.[8]

It's true that if we want to see each other clearly then we have to look right into the heart of the moment. Kiều looked, and she was able to see very deeply. She could see the dragons and clouds in Từ Hải's future.[9] She could see his great heart and his deepest aspiration. Have you truly seen your beloved? Has your beloved truly seen you?

Looking at one another deeply, we can see each other's deepest aspirations.[10]

When we understand
each other's deepest aspirations,
we become soulmates.

now and
when?

That Moment Is Now

The now can be the most beautiful moment. It's so beautiful that you can hardly believe it's real.

But reality is as it is. The present moment is more beautiful than any kind of dream. This moment is no dream. This is reality. Pinch yourself—doesn't it hurt? You are not dreaming. You are fully awake. You have had so many dreams, but no dream is as beautiful as the reality that is unfolding itself to you in the here and the now.

Mother Earth is a bodhisattva of infinite beauty. Mother Earth has never been as beautiful as she is now. We may be inspired to write poem after poem in her praise. Every one of her four seasons is beautiful. Yet there is no poet, no painter, no composer, no architect, no mathematician as talented as Mother Earth herself. Mother Earth is the mother of all buddhas and bodhisattvas. She is the mother of all saints and holy people. A white crane, a limpid creek, a cherry tree in blossom, a serene moonlit night, a mighty snow-capped peak—all bear witness to her splendor.

Mother Earth has brought you to life and she is you. You are as beautiful as she is, because you are her. Your nature is her nature—the nature of no birth, no death, no coming, no going, no being, no nonbeing, no sameness, no otherness. You are the green willow, you are the yellow chrysanthemum, you are the red rose, you are the violet bamboo swaying in the wind.

You are invited to come back to the now, and you will be in touch with her. You will find in this very moment everything that you have ever been looking for.

The now embraces all the whens
and all the might have beens.

With awe I realize that long-awaited moment is now.

I see clearly all before me, but still suspect it is a dream.[11]

Kiều's family finally finds her after fifteen years of separation, fifteen years of untold suffering and despair. Kiều had been taken far from home and, unable to return, had given up hope of ever seeing her family again. She simply cannot believe her eyes when they suddenly appear. Kiều cannot believe that the moment she's been dreaming of for so long is here, now.

Every moment is like that, if we can see it clearly. You discover that the present moment, this very now, is already more beautiful than you could ever have imagined. You doubt that it's real because it's so unbelievably beautiful; you think you must be dreaming. What more are you looking for? What more do you need to attain? You already are what you want to become. You already have everything you need to be happy.

There is no way to the Pure Land; the Pure Land is the way. There is no way to the Kingdom of God; the Kingdom is the way. The Pure Land and the Kingdom are available in every step.

There is no Pure Land,
there is no Kingdom outside of the now.

Only When...

Dear one, do not seek happiness in the future. Do not wait for that day, do not wait for a distant future *then* . . . Do not say that happiness will be possible *only when* you have this or that. What is it you are looking for? What is it you are waiting for? Is it fame? Is it wealth? Is it power? Is it sex? Or is it just distraction from the emptiness inside? Do not think that you will be truly happy *only when* you have obtained these things. Do not wait for *then*.

Look around. There are plenty of people who have all of these things, but they do not have peace of mind, they are still not happy. They never feel they have enough because the well of desire is bottomless. If we are thirsty but we keep eating salt, we will only get more and more thirsty. We need to know the practices of *having as few desires as possible* and of "I have enough." When we can see that in this very moment *we already have enough*, our thirst is quenched, our craving is calmed, and true happiness becomes possible.

At one moment in *The Tale of Kiều* the brave warrior Từ Hải confides to Kiều that, even though he loves her deeply, he feels they cannot go on living together quietly forever. "All we have now is each other," he says. "I haven't yet made a name for myself, I haven't made my fortune. I need to make my way in the world, to achieve something truly great. *Only when* I have a hundred thousand troops under my command and can welcome you home as my queen will I be truly happy."

Because of this *only when*, Từ Hải decides to leave Kiều alone for an entire year. She begs him to let her accompany him on his journey, but he refuses.

When a hundred thousand men have I,

When drums and banners shake the earth, shadow the sky,

When all around acknowledge my greatness,

Only then will I again receive you by my side.[12]

Our beloved ones are there. They are our partner, our friend, our child, or our parent. And yet we have the feeling that just being together is not enough; we need something more. We feel the need to go out in search of success, achievement, more money, or more status to bring back to offer our dear ones in order to make them happy, to make them proud, to earn their love. The *then* becomes the condition of the *now*.

Many of us think that only once we have this or that, only once the situation changes, only *then* can we be happy. We do not recognize our happiness in the *now*, and we seek it in the *then*. We have the idea that happiness lies in some future moment. We say to one another, "We have to wait, my beloved, and *then* . . . " And while we busy ourselves trying to bring about that *then*, we abandon our loved ones in the *now*. We sacrifice the *now* which is so precious, for the *then* which never comes.

The then always belongs to the future.
It is an illusion that can never become reality.

Looking in the Same Direction

Someone said that to love each other is not just to sit there and look at each other, but to look in the same direction.[13] Is this true? If we both look in the same direction, what then is that direction? Is it the direction of power, fame, and wealth? That would mean that our love alone does not satisfy us—our love is not enough for our happiness. If that direction is the direction of the television, then that is truly a tragedy.

In the beginning, when we first fell in love, we only needed to look at each other to be happy. Now, looking at each other we are no longer happy, because we have hurt each other so many times. Looking at the television is just a way of covering up the suffering and the loneliness each of us feels inside.

If the direction we are looking in is the direction of our ideals, of our deepest aspirations, then what are our ideals, our aspirations? Clearly they're not fame or wealth—because those are not true ideals. And yet very often ideals that appear beautiful may conceal within them a deeper desire for fame and profit. We deceive ourselves; we deceive others. We deceive ourselves with the good, the true, the beautiful; with justice, equality, and brotherhood; with humanism or socialism.

Why do we not feel at peace just sitting and looking at each other? Looking at each other we discover the wonders of each other, and we learn to treasure each other. Looking at each other we recognize the wonders of the here and the now. Looking at each other we can see each other's concerns and aspirations, as well as each other's fears, suffering, and loneliness. When we see and understand the pain and the suffering in ourselves and in the other person, understanding and compassion in us begin to grow. These are the energies that have the power to heal and transform us. This is the secret to nourishing our love. When we look at the world, we see that nothing can survive without food. The same is true with love. However beautiful our love is, it is impermanent. We need to learn how to feed our love with the energy of understanding and compassion. Only when we know how to look deeply at each other, and how to look deeply at ourselves, can we generate these two precious energies.

When we know how to nourish our love, we can heal ourselves and heal those around us. When love grows, it naturally embraces more and more. If your love is true love, then it will continue to grow until it includes all people and all species. Your love will become a river, wide enough to nourish not only you and your beloved, but the whole world. This is love without limits, a heart without boundaries, and without discrimination. It is unlimited compassion, unlimited loving kindness. It brings joy to everyone. Nothing and no one is excluded from this love—that is why it is called the love of limitless inclusiveness.

Love that doesn't grow is love that is already beginning to die. That is why we should look at each other deeply—to help our love grow. Looking into the suffering of our beloved one, we will see the suffering of all living beings and our compassion will begin to grow. Our compassion will become as powerful as thunder, and our loving kindness will be like the rain—refreshing drops that can penetrate into the hearts of all beings. A cloud may look very gentle and soft, but it can produce powerful thunder.

True love is never weak.
Great compassion is also great courage.

Dwell Peacefully

If you are restless, if you are not able to sit peacefully and with stability, it is because you are not established in the now. Restlessness is the disease of our times, and the more we try to fill it with the consumption of things—such as food and drink, movies, websites, books, or games—the more the emptiness grows and the more restless we become. We should remind each other that the now is the only thing that is solid and real.

The now is a remarkable, fascinating, and beautiful place—the foundation of all time and space.

All you need to do is to focus your attention on your in-breath and out-breath, recognize it, and smile to it. Being aware that you are breathing in means you are really there. Your presence is a wonder and a miracle. Breathing like that, you bring your mind back to your body and become truly present in the now. Treasuring that moment, you dwell in peace and freedom. Each breath is a miracle. Each breath has the power to nourish and to heal.

Breathing mindfully, dwelling in peace and freedom, you see yourself as the wondrous *Dharmakaya*, you see yourself as the lover of the cosmos.[14] You see yourself as Mother Earth and Father Sun.

Walking in the Now

If when you walk you are harried or discontented, and your steps are not solid, it is because you are still searching for something in the past or in the future. You are not aware that what you are searching for is already there in the present moment. If each step you make brings you back to the present, then that step will become as solid as Mother Earth herself. Making a step like that, it's as though a lotus is blooming under your foot. You walk in freedom, peace, and contentment. You will be one of the most beautiful people on Earth, thanks to your ability to dwell peacefully in the now.

You don't need to look for anything else, because you yourself are the object of all searching. If you have not realized this yet, then even though everything around you may be peaceful and safe, you still will not feel safe and at ease. Looking at the beautiful, silent moon you will wonder why your heart is still not at peace.

Some people possess something very special: they have the now in their heart. When we have a chance to sit close to such a person, we feel so peaceful. They radiate an energy of peace that penetrates us deeply. Whenever we have a chance to walk alongside them, we can feel this subtle source of peace and joy. Their steps are peaceful and free, and that helps us to walk with peace and freedom.

You too can walk like this. Walk as if you do not need to get anywhere—as if you are arriving with every step. Each step can bring you back to the island within— back to the wonderful present moment, back to the now.

Walking together like this, we feel like drops of water flowing in a vast and gentle river. The drop of water does not need to do anything. The drop is embraced by the river and transported to the ocean of the present moment.

Drinking Clouds

Every time you drink your tea, you have an eternity to enjoy drinking your tea. The clouds stop running, the wind stops flying, and time stands still. The clouds are present in your tea. The wind is present in your tea. I am also in your tea.

Drink your tea as if you are drinking clouds.

long have
i sought

What Are You Looking For?

If long beneath the sea I sought a pin,

Was it for love's true gold, or only the fickle flowers and moon of lust?[15]

You have been searching for something, my dear one. Searching for so long in vain. It's as though you've been looking for a needle at the bottom of the ocean. What is it you've been looking for? Were you looking for just another fleeting illusion of happiness—or were you looking for true love? Yes, the love you are looking for is the love of solid rock and gold—true love—not mere lust and sensual pleasure.

What is true love? Where can you find it? Are you able to find understanding and love within you? Do you really need for *someone else* to love and understand you? If you are so starved of love and understanding, then who will ever be able to understand and love you?

If you cannot understand yourself, if you cannot love yourself, how will you ever be able to understand or love another person? And how will you ever allow another person to love you?

After years of searching, Kim Trọng finally finds his true love Kiều far from home. Fifteen years have slipped away since their one magical day together, when they pledged their deep vow of eternal love to one another under the light of the moon. Kiều has been saved from taking her own life and is now a nun. Although she has suffered so much, she has been able to learn a lot from her suffering. Perhaps now she even understands life and death better than the learned scholar Kim Trọng. After giving up all hope of being reunited, Kiều's joy is now immeasurable. But the peace and purity she has now attained is so precious to her that she is adamant they must keep their love as pure and unconsummated as it was on that moonlit night. She is able to help Kim Trọng realize that if his love has endured all these years of searching, it was not because of the fleeting passions of lust, but because of something much deeper and more precious—the solid gold of true love.

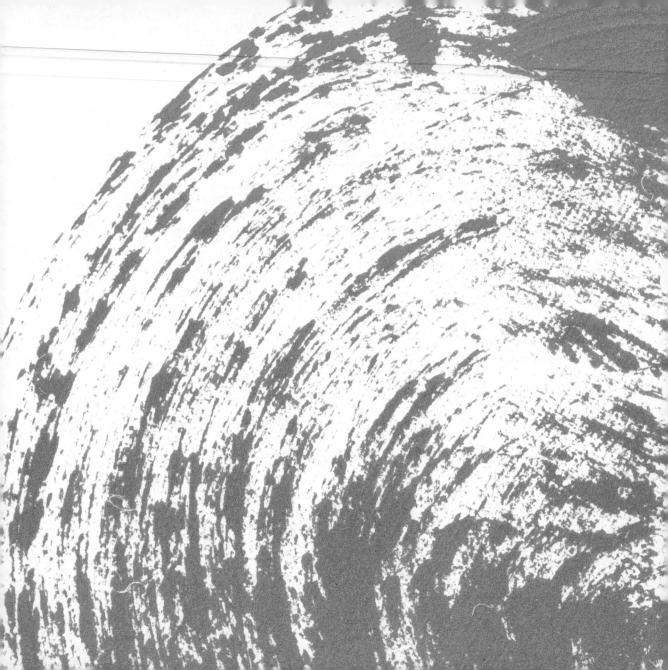

The Magic Spyglass

In order to recognize your true love, you will need a magic spyglass. With this spyglass, you will be able to recognize your soulmate. Without it, you wouldn't be able to recognize your soulmate even if he or she were sitting right in front of you.

Your magic spyglass is something you make yourself, with your *kung fu*, your daily practice. You have to listen to yourself. You need to recognize the suffering within you—and to see the ways it carries within itself the suffering of your father, your mother, your ancestors, and your people. As you come to understand the suffering within you, the energy of compassion will be born in your heart. It will calm you and begin to heal you. You will feel light and peaceful.

True love has the power to heal and transform.

Embracing your suffering and listening to it,

you will start to understand it.

You will find the roots of your anxiety and be able to identify your deepest aspiration. You will see yourself more clearly, understand yourself better, and become your own true love. This is the magic spyglass that will allow you to recognize your beloved, your soulmate, the one you have always been searching for.

this is it

·This Is It

For so long have I awaited this day.[16]

The opportunity that you have been waiting for is right here in the present moment. Each step is that opportunity; each breath is that opportunity—an opportunity for you to go back to the now and stop your endless wandering and *waiting for that day to come.*

The day that you've been waiting for is today;
the moment that you've been waiting for
is this very moment.

You must pierce the veil of time and space in order to come to the here and the now.

No matter what your circumstances are, that opportunity is there for you. In the now, you will find what you have been looking for.

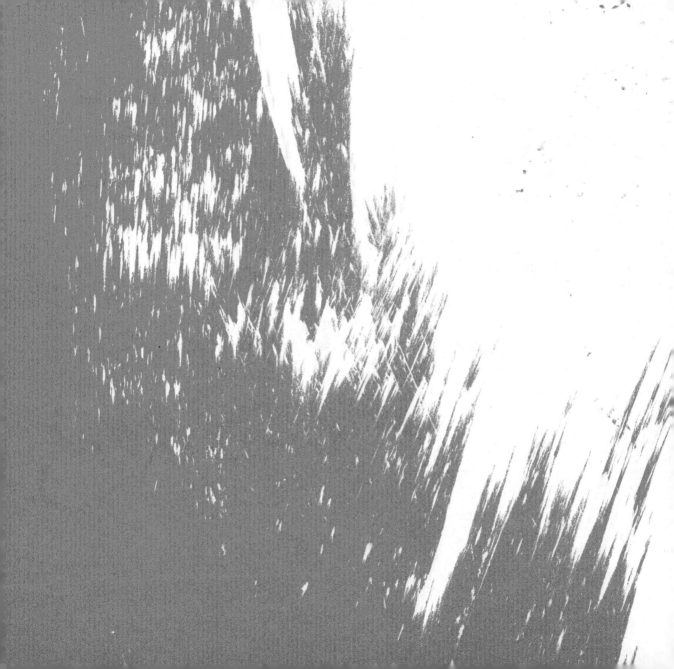

Heaven yet preserves for us this day

We Still Have The Now

Please do not say that the moment has passed, that now it is too late. Perhaps in the past there were difficulties between you and your loved one, divisive words, and mistaken perceptions. You were not able to see each other clearly and recognize each other's true presence. These obstacles are the clouds that shroud the moon, the mist that obscures the flowers. You think that everything has fallen apart—that the moon has waned, the flowers have withered, and that you have lost each other.

But in the present moment, with the energy of mindfulness and concentration, you will be able to clear away the misunderstandings, the anger, the sadness, and suspicion of days gone by. It is exactly in this very moment, today, that the work must be done. You are still alive! Treasure the reality that you are still alive. Do not allow your afflictions, craving, anger, and despair to overwhelm you. Live the moment that life is offering you. Sit down quietly and meditate to look deeply and sweep away the wild imaginings, the prejudices, and the wrong perceptions of the past. Part the clouds and uncover the brightly shining moon in the vast sky; dissolve the mist to find the dazzling flowers and fresh new buds.

You still have each other. Nothing has passed away and nothing is lost. That is because the now is still with us—because today is still here. The moon will be brighter than it was, the flowers fresher than before, because now you know how to pierce the veil of mist at the gate and roll back the clouds to reveal the vast open sky. Life is still there, waiting for us this very day, more so than ever before.

This day today is still everything.

Heaven yet preserves for us this day,

Mist melts from the gate, clouds furl up in the sky,

Flowers once withered are fresher now than ever before,

The waned moon now brighter still than moons of yore. [17]

not a creation
but a
manifestation

Interbeing

Beloved one, you are not something that has been created—you did not come into the realm of being from the realm of nonbeing. You are a wonderful manifestation, like a pink cloud on the top of a mountain, or a mysterious moonlit night. You are a flowing stream, the continuation of so many wonders. You are not a separate self. You are yourself, but you are also me. You cannot take the pink cloud out of my fragrant tea this morning. And I cannot drink my tea without drinking my cloud.

I am in you and you are in me. If we take me out of you, then you would not be able to manifest as you are manifesting now. If we take you out of me, I would not be able to manifest as I am manifesting now. We cannot manifest without one another. We have to wait for each other in order to manifest together.

In the Bible it is said that God gave the command, "Let there be light!"

I imagine the light must have replied, "But I have to wait, my Lord."

"What are you waiting for?" God asked.

"I am waiting for the darkness so that we can manifest together."

"But darkness is already there," said God.

"In that case," said the light, "I am already there, too."

We cannot exist, we cannot *be*, by ourselves alone. We can only *inter-be*, like the left and the right, above and below, good and evil, creator and created. The lover and the beloved are of the same nature, they manifest at the same time. There cannot be a lover if there is no one to love. You cannot take one out of the other, just as you cannot take the left out of the right, the inside out of the outside. Both the lover and the beloved are, by nature, empty.

A flower is made only of non-flower elements. A Buddha is made only of non-Buddha elements. The one who bows and the one who is bowed to are contained within each other.[18] That is why, my beloved one, you should know that your beloved is already in you. You should not try to look for him or for her outside yourself. You are empty; that is why love is possible. If there is no emptiness, then there is nothing at all.

It is only thanks to emptiness that everything can manifest. Self-nature is an illusion.

The Happiest Moment in Your Life

Has the happiest moment of your life come yet? If the most fulfilling, uplifting moment of exaltation has already happened once, it can happen many times more. But how can we help that moment come more often, especially when we want it to? If in the last thirty years that moment has not come, then it's not likely to come in the next thirty years and perhaps it never will. Don't just dream about it. The secret is to produce that moment ourselves. When? Right in this moment.

You need to *wake up*! Wake up to the wonders within you and around you. If you know the way, then any moment of your life can become the happiest moment of your life.

Dear one, please come, and lean your arms on this windowsill. Look out. Do you see the wonderful immensity of space in front of you? Do you see the vast blue ocean? Can you see the wings of the seagull playing with the sunlight? Looking out, you see immensity; but looking in, you also see immensity. The world inside is as vast as the world outside. In fact, reality transcends both the notions of inside and outside. This special window is everywhere—it is in you and in me. It helps us to see the miraculous world of no birth and no death, no coming and no going.

there are times
i climb to the
mountain top

On Top of the World

The Zen Master Không Lộ found a wonderful place to live in the mountains where he could enjoy the wilderness day and night.[19] There were times when he would climb up to the top of a nearby mountain peak. Standing there all alone, he would let forth a wild yell.

The whole cosmos responds to that yell; and the sound freezes the whole cosmos. It is a wonderful moment, a most fulfilling moment, a most satisfying moment. Any moment can be a moment like that if you know how to handle the now, if you have the time, and if you take the opportunity.

有時值上 高頂

長呌一聲寒太虛

Không Lộ had limitless time and countless opportunities, because he had the now.

Every one of his moments was an opportunity.

There are times I climb to the mountain top,

and let forth a howl that freezes the cosmos.[20]

There are times . . . which times? *Being Time* . . . what time?

Each moment can be all the moments;

each moment is an opportunity waiting to be seized.

Không Lộ's yell is still reverberating—it is still heard now and for all eternity.

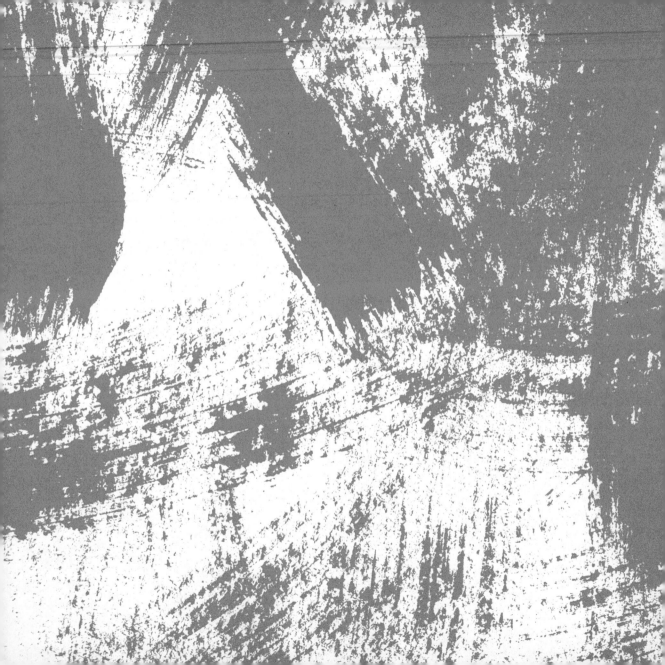

古佛言

有時高高峯頂立、

有時深深海底行、

有時三頭八臂、

有時丈六八尺、

有時拄杖払子、

有時露柱灯餛、

有時張三李四、

有時大地虛空

Time is for Being

Dōgen begins his poem "Being Time" with these lines:

A former Buddha once said in verse:

There is a time I stand on top of a soaring mountain peak

There is a time I walk in the deepest ocean abyss

There is a time I have three heads and eight arms

There is a time I have a golden body, eight or sixteen feet tall

There is a time I am a monk's staff or fly whisk

There is a time I am a pillar or a stone lantern

There is a time I am a certain Mr. Dupont or Mr. Smith

There is a time I am the vast sky and the great Earth [21]

Being
time

Who is the ancient Buddha mentioned by Dōgen? And what does it mean, "there is a time?" Each line begins with the characters 有時, "being time," meaning, "there is a time," or, "there are times."

To be standing on the peak of a mountain and let forth a wild yell that shakes the heavens—that is so wonderful. To be a deity with three heads and eight arms as often seen in the Hindu tradition can be equally wonderful. And to be a Buddha with a golden body of sixteen feet is marvellous. But to be a pillar or a lantern? To be you or me, or to be a certain Monsieur Dupont or Mister Smith? Yes, it is equally wonderful. Because the Kingdom of God can be found in even the tiniest flower, in a bullfrog, or in the mud that nourishes the lotus.

To see oneself as the vast sky and great Earth is to attain nirvana, the ground of no birth and no death.

Time is for being, and for being anything.

When you see the mountain, you are the mountain, the mountain is you. The mountain is time. The mountain is the now. In Sanskrit, the word for "now" is *drstādharma*, "that which is now being seen."

When you see the great Earth, you are the great Earth. The great Earth is time. The great Earth is the now.

You cannot take anything out of anything.

enjoying
space
outside of
space

Space Outside of Space

Zen Master Không Lộ and Zen Master Dōgen both possess the now, and so they also have the here. Not only do they enjoy the here and the now, but they are *themselves* the here and the now. Time, space, matter, and consciousness are not four separate things.

When you learn to live in the now, you see that your being can be limited neither by the space of a physical body nor by the time of a life span. If the world of a person were only one hundred years, then even the sky seen from Không Lộ's peak could never be vast enough. But when you live deeply the now, you have the opportunity to liberate yourself from time and enter time outside of time, and space outside of space.[22]

Chorus

I will never grow up

no matter how long I live.

Just yesterday, I saw a band

of golden butterflies fluttering above our garden.

The mustard greens were bursting with bright yellow flowers.

Mother and sister, you are always with me.

The gentle afternoon breeze is your breathing.

I am not dreaming of some distant future.

I am back. Someone is singing.

My hand touches the old gate,

and I ask, "What can I do to help?"

The wind replies,

"Smile. Life is a miracle.

Be a flower.

Happiness is not built of bricks and stones."

My mother's hair is fresh and long.

It touches her heels.

The dress my sister hangs out to dry

is still sailing in the wind

over our green yard.

It was an Autumn morning

with a light breeze.

I am really standing in our backyard—

the guava trees, the fragrance of ripe mangoes,

the red maple leaves scurrying about

like little children at our feet.

A song drifts from across the river.

Bales of silky, golden hay

traverse the bamboo bridge.

Such fragrance!

As the moon rises above

the bamboo thicket,

we play together

near the front gate.

I am not dreaming.

This is a real day, a beautiful one.

Do we want to return to the past

and play hide-and-seek?
We are here today,
and we will be here tomorrow.
This is true.

Come, you are thirsty.

We can walk together

to the spring of fresh water.

The chrysanthemum is smiling to you.

Don't dip your hands into cement and sand.

The stars never build prisons for themselves.

Let us sing with the flower and the morning birds.

Let us be fully present.

I know you are here because I can look into your eyes.

And bring mother. I want to see her.

I will sing for you, my dear sister,

and your hair will grow as long as mother's. [23]

NOTES

1. The first pilot project of the SYSS was started in January 1964. Living there were the Venerable nun Tịnh Nguyện, the novice Nhất Trí, sisters Trà Mi, Phương Thải, Phùng Thăng, and Cao Ngọc Thanh, and the brothers Lê Khắc Tích and Tâm Quang. From September 1964 onward, there was sister Phượng, and brothers Trần Tấn Trâm, Lê Thành Nguyên, and Hồ văn Quyền. The year 1965 was the first year we began to enroll students, and in September the first term began for the SYSS as a branch of the Vạn Hạnh Institute of Education.

2. The Tale of Kiều is considered to be the supreme achievement of Vietnamese literature. Written in the early nineteenth century, the story is known by all Vietnamese people, memorized in its entirety by some, and often quoted in everyday conversation. In 1,627 spare couplets, the author vividly brings to life a story of love, fate, and tragedy, which is at the same time a biting commentary on the turbulent political situation of Vietnam at the turn of the eighteenth century. The poem is rich in allusions and references to classical Chinese literature while also celebrating the richness and depth of the Vietnamese language in all its diversity of rhythm and tone.

Kiều is a beautiful and talented young girl who falls in love with a handsome scholar, Kim Trọng. They are separated just after they have pledged troth to each other, and she is forced to sell herself into marriage with an older man in order to save her family from destitution.

She discovers to her horror that she has been tricked and has been married to a pimp. She is first saved from the brothel by a weak-willed young man who falls passionately in love with her and arranges for her escape. But he is already married, and his wife plots revenge on Kiều. She briefly becomes a nun but the wife's plot eventually forces her back into prostitution. She is only released when the young hero Từ Hải recognizes in her a kindred soul and buys back her freedom. They have a short period of happiness before he leaves her to make his name. He returns as a powerful rebel general and he sends out in search of all her former tormentors to mete out justice. Some are forgiven and some are executed. Kiều later persuades him to put down his arms and give himself up to the king's men, in order to save the lives of many thousands of soldiers; but he is betrayed and killed. Devastated, Kiều tries to commit suicide in a river but is saved from drowning by the nun Giác Duyên, her friend and mentor. She ordains as a nun for the second time and, fifteen years after she was first sold away, is finally reunited with her family and with her first love, Kim Trọng.

Her family persuades her to honor her original pledge to Kim Trọng and perform a marriage ceremony with him, but she pleads with him not to sully the purity of their love with sensual desire, and she lives out the rest of her life peacefully in chastity. There is a bilingual Vietnamese and English edition of The Tale of Kiều by Nguyễn Du available from Yale University Press (New Haven, 1987).

3. Dōgen Zenji was a Japanese Zen Buddhist teacher born in Kyōto in the thirteenth century. He founded the Sōtō school of Zen in Japan after travelling to China where he lived for several years while receiving training at a number of Chan monasteries. He wrote prolifically and his most famous work is called the *Shōbōgenzō*. It is broken up into ninety-five shorter pieces or episodes. The piece focusing on the nature of impermanence and time, called the "Uji," translates from Japanese into something like "for the time being" or "being time." Dōgen wrote "Uji" in the early winter of 1240 when he was forty-one years old. The trilingual edition that inspired Thay is *Uji, être-temps (Being-Time)* by Dōgen, translated by Eidō Shimano and Charles Vacher (Paris: Encre Marine, 1997).

4. *Niệm Phật thị thuỳ?—Who is the one reciting the Buddha's name?* One of the most widely used koans in the Chinese Zen school.

5. *Đến bây giờ mới thấy đây, mà lòng đã chắc những ngày một hai (Tale of Kiều,* lines 2283–2284). We may rewrite the first line, inserting the implied words: Đến [được cái] *bây giờ* [thì] *mới thấy* [được cái ở] *đây,* which in English gives, *Arriving at the now, we begin to see the here.*

6. Opening verse from *Auguries of Innocence,* William Blake, 1803. Blake's lines are very similar to those written by Vietnamese Zen Master Khánh Hỷ (1067–1142) during the Lý Dynasty: *All Heaven and Earth balanced on the tip of a hair, Both Sun and Moon in a mustard seed contained—. Càn khôn tận thị mao đầu thượng, nhật nguyệt bao hàm giới tử trung.*

7. *Bây giờ rõ mặt đôi ta, biết đâu rồi nữa chẳng là chiêm bao? (Tale of Kiều,* lines 443–444).

8. *Lại đây, xem lại cho gần (Tale of Kiều,* line 2195). Từ Hải has heard rumours of Kiều''s beauty and seeks her out in the pleasure-house where she has been captured for a second time in prostitution. He is immediately smitten, and assures her how fortunate she is to have found a real man who will take care of her as she deserves. But, trapped and powerless, Kiều retorts that although she craves to be able entrust her heart to someone, she does not have that kind of freedom. He begs her to look him in the eye, closely, to see for herself what kind of man he is.

9. *Tấn Dương được thấy mây rồng có phen. Tấn Dương shall see a dragon in the clouds (Tale of Kiều,* line 2198). When Kiều looks into Từ Hải's eyes she sees the clouds and dragons of *Tấn Dương.* This deeply auspicious sign makes reference to a prophecy made about the brilliant imperial future of a four-year-old boy in seventh-century China. He grew up to be a powerful rebel general and succeeded in establishing the T'ang Imperial Dynasty.

10. *Nghe lời vừa ý gật đầu, cười rằng "tri kỷ trước sau mấy người?" (Tale of Kiều,* lines 2201–2202). *Hearing Kiều's words he nodded with pleasure, And smiling said, "How many in life can see another's soul?"* In their intense first encounter, Từ Hải

recognizes that Kiều is the only person to have ever truly seen and understood him. He falls deeply in love and soon buys her freedom from prostitution. He has found his soulmate.

11. *Ngỡ bây giờ là bao giờ, rõ ràng trước mắt còn ngờ chiêm bao* (*Tale of Kiều*, lines 3015–3016). Kiều has been separated from her family and her first love, Kim Trọng, for fifteen years, since she first sold herself away in order to save her father from the debtor's prison. Twice she has been sold into prostitution, twice a slave. At every opportunity she has tried to escape and return to her family but, alone and strikingly beautiful, she does not get far before she is caught and deceived again.

After her great love, hero, and protector Từ Hải, was tragically betrayed and killed in part because of her, Kiều threw herself into the river to drown. She is rescued by a nun and they live quietly together in a temple by the river. Kiều enjoys the peace but is bitterly homesick and fears that she will never see her family again. But hearing of the end of the war, Kiều's family and Kim Trọng set off in search of her

Rumors take them to the river where she is said to have drowned, and there they finally find Kiều living as a nun. When Kiều sees them coming, she cannot believe her eyes. That moment is too good to be true. Every night for fifteen years, she had dreamed of being reunited, and every night she had despaired of ever finding her family again. Now, in this moment, suddenly all those who she loves the most in the world are right there in front of her. It is the moment she has been dreaming of, and she cannot believe it's true. *Ngỡ bây giờ là bao giờ—With awe I realize that long-awaited moment is* now, is a most wonderful phrase.

12. *Bao giờ mười vạn tinh binh, Tiếng chiêng dậy đất, bóng tinh rợp đường, Làm cho tỏ mặt phi thường, Bấy giờ ta mới rước nàng nghi gia* (*Tale of Kiều*, lines 2223–2226). Từ Hải abandons Kiều to seek fame and glory, ignoring her pleas to let her accompany him.

13. *L'expérience nous montre qu'aimer ce n'est point nous regarder l'un l'autre mais regarder ensemble dans la même direction—Experience shows us that to love is not just to look at each other, but to be looking out together in the same direction.* From *Wind, Sand, and Stars*, Antoine de St-Exupéry, 1939.

14. *Dharmakaya* literally means the "body" (*kaya*) of the Buddha's teachings (*Dharma*), the way of understanding and love. In Mahayana Buddhism the words have come to mean "the essence of all that exists." To see yourself as the Dharmakaya means to see yourself as one with the cosmos.

15. *Bấy lâu đáy bể mò kim, là nhiều vàng đá phải tìm trăng hoa?* (*Tale of Kiều*, lines 3177–3178).

16. *Bấy lâu mới được một ngày* (*Tale of Kiều*, line 315). Since the first time he caught a glimpse of the young, beautiful, and innocent Kiều, Kim Trọng has longed for the day he can see her again. Now that long-awaited moment has come, and he persuades her to stay and talk to him.

17. *Trời còn để có hôm nay, tan sương đầu ngõ, vén mây giữa trời. Hoa tàn mà lại thêm tươi, trăng tàn mà lại hơn mười rằm xưa* (Tale of Kiều, lines 3123–3126). Reunited at last, Kim Trọng tries to persuade Kiều that it is not too late to realize their vow pledged under the glowing moon and enjoy deep happiness together. They still have this moment; nothing has been lost. The moon is still as bright, and their love still as fresh as it ever was.

18. *The one who bows and the one who is bowed to are both by nature empty.* This is the first line of a verse which is recited by monks and nuns in the Buddhist tradition before bowing to the Buddha. Everyone, including the Buddha is full of the whole cosmos, and empty of only one thing: a separate self. To say a person is "empty" is to say they are empty of a separate self.

19. The twelfth-century Vietnamese Zen Master Không Lộ belonged to the tenth generation of the Vô Ngôn Thông lineage, and he passed away in 1141.

20. These are two lines from a poem by Zen Master Không Lộ. The phrase "there are times," or "being time," is made up of two Chinese characters, 有時, which is also the title of Dōgen's famous essay written in 1240, a century later. Both Không Lộ in the twelfth century, and Dōgen in the thirteenth century, took the phrase, 有時, "being time," as their inspiration.

21. This eight-line verse is by Chinese Master Yao Shan.

22. The famous thirteenth-century Vietnamese Zen Master Tuệ Trung wrote a beautiful poem about enjoying "space outside of space" (*phương ngoại phương*). He was a member of the great dynastic family of Trần, but he chose to withdraw from court life and live in a hermitage where he could devote himself entirely to spiritual practice. He became a great lay Zen master and poet. In one of his most beautiful and simple verses, he describes how he would take up his bamboo staff, set out from his little hut, and climb the mountain to "go and enjoy space outside of space" (*Trượng tích ưu du hề, phương ngoại phương*).

23. Excerpted from "Butterflies over the Golden Mustard Fields," Thich Nhat Hanh, 1963. See *Call Me By My True Names: The Collected Poems of Thich Nhat Hanh* (Berkeley: Parallax Press, 1999).

PARALLAX
PRESS

Parallax Press is a nonprofit publisher, founded and inspired by Zen Master Thich Nhat Hanh. We publish books on mindfulness in daily life and are committed to making these teachings accessible to everyone and preserving them for future generation. We do this work to alleviate suffering and contribute to a more just and joyful world.

Parallax Press
P.O. Box 7355
Berkeley, CA 94707
Tel: (510) 540-6411
parallax.org

Monastics and laypeople practice the art of mindful living in the tradition of Thich Nhat Hanh
at retreat communities worldwide. To reach any of these communities, or for information about individuals
and families joining for a practice period, please contact:

Plum Village
13 Martineau
33580 Dieulivol, France
plumvillage.org

Blue Cliff Monastery
3 Mindfulness Road
Pine Bush, NY 12566
bluecliffmonastery.org

Magnolia Grove Monastery
123 Towles Rd.
Batesville, MS 38606
magnoliagrovemonastery.org

Deer Park Monastery
2499 Melru Lane
Escondido, CA 92026
deerparkmonastery.org

The Mindfulness Bell, a journal of the art of mindful living in the tradition of Thich Nhat Hanh,
is published three times a year by Plum Village. To subscribe or to see the worldwide directory of Sanghas, visit
mindfulnessbell.org.